JOHN LALL

TAJ MAHAL

AND THE SAGA OF THE GREAT MUGHALS

Lustre Press

Delhi ◇ Banaras ◇ Agra ◇ Jaipur ◇ The Netherlands

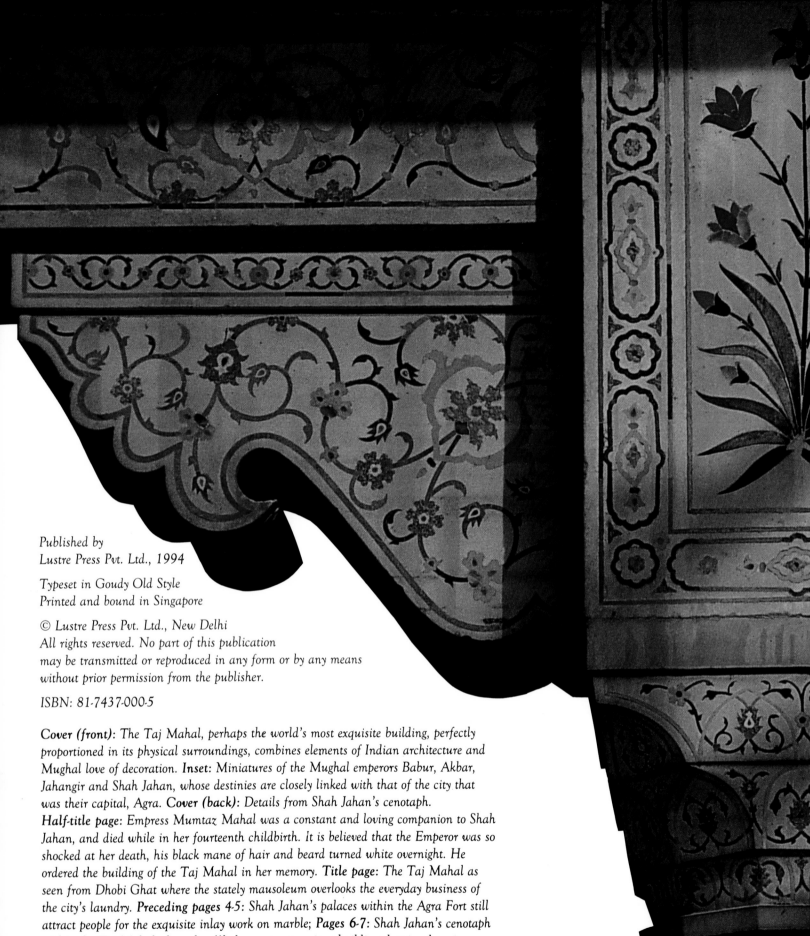

Published by
Lustre Press Pvt. Ltd., 1994

Typeset in Goudy Old Style
Printed and bound in Singapore

ISBN: 81-7437-000-5

Cover (front): The Taj Mahal, perhaps the world's most exquisite building, perfectly proportioned in its physical surroundings, combines elements of Indian architecture and Mughal love of decoration. **Inset:** Miniatures of the Mughal emperors Babur, Akbar, Jahangir and Shah Jahan, whose destinies are closely linked with that of the city that was their capital, Agra. **Cover (back):** Details from Shah Jahan's cenotaph.
Half-title page: Empress Mumtaz Mahal was a constant and loving companion to Shah Jahan, and died while in her fourteenth childbirth. It is believed that the Emperor was so shocked at her death, his black mane of hair and beard turned white overnight. He ordered the building of the Taj Mahal in her memory. **Title page:** The Taj Mahal as seen from Dhobi Ghat where the stately mausoleum overlooks the everyday business of the city's laundry. **Preceding pages 4-5:** Shah Jahan's palaces within the Agra Fort still attract people for the exquisite inlay work on marble; **Pages 6-7:** Shah Jahan's cenotaph within the Taj Mahal, the only off-balance structure in a building that is otherwise perfectly proportioned; **Pages 8-9:** Looking out above the ramparts of the Agra Fort; **Pages 10-11:** On a bend of the river Yamuna, the Taj Mahal is perfectly located, and faces the Agra Fort that was Shah Jahan's capital for the Mughal empire even though he was to build the Red Fort in Delhi, and his predecessors had ruled from Lahore and Fatehpur Sikri.

CONTENTS

This page: Detail from a column at Agra Fort. The art of pietra dura inlay was encouraged by Empress Nur Jahan, but proved most successful during the reign of her stepson, Shah Jahan. Overleaf: A reflection of Mughal taste, when everything from silver slippers to jade inlay was characterised with attention to detail. On these pages are inlaid boxes, snuff and opium containers of jade inlaid with emeralds and rubies, footwear in silver, a locket with its hidden container, and a pen stand in the shape of a peacock-boat. Pages 16 and 17: Scenes from the Babur Nama.

ظهیرالدین بابر پادشاه نمبر ۶

The Great Mughal Dynasty

The arrival of Babur in Hindustan marked a shift of fortunes in the history of the nation.
For Babur was to found a dynasty whose three-hundred-year reign in Delhi and Agra
would leave behind a heritage that, centuries later, continues to represent
an architectural, cultural and administrative climax for the Indian subcontinent.

*A*GRA BECAME the backdrop of the glorious Mughal pageant by one of those obscure occurrences which are the fascination of history. For nearly a thousand years Delhi has been the capital of India, from being the seat of the famed Prithviraj Chauhan and five dynasties of Muslim Sultans, from the Slave kings of the thirteenth century to the Lodis of the fifteenth and sixteenth. It remained the capital of the later Mughals until the British sent the last figurehead Mughal emperor into exile after the Revolt of 1857. Tradition brought the British back to Delhi at the great Durbar of 1911, and it remains today the capital of independent India.

Even though it houses some of the most exquisite specimens of Mughal architecture, Agra has never been at the hub of Indian history, Mughal or otherwise. It has had its moments of glory and some of these have left indelible marks on the landscape of the city, so that in spite of its having always played second fiddle the claims of Agra can never be ignored.

We first hear of Agra some time in 1504 when Sikander Lodi, based at Delhi, sailed down the river Yamuna, that connects Delhi with Agra, to occupy the old Rajput fort of Badalgarh. A revolt had been brewing against Sikander in the large tract south of Agra and the Sultan found Delhi too distant to

Facing page : Emperor Babur, the founder of the Mughal dynasty in India, who assumed kingship of Hindustan in 1526. He was the first Mughal to rule from Agra and his citadel was the medieval Rajput fortress, Badalgarh. **Above** : *A 'tabeez' or locket in 'kundan' work, a Rajput legacy from Rajasthan that found favour with the Mughals.*

conduct operations against the rebels. Thus, Agra became the temporary capital of the Lodis.

The secondary status for Agra was to continue under many future kings, chiefly the Mughals, and would be institutionalised in the fine distinction that Abu'l-Fazl—the scribe, courtier and biographer in the court of Akbar, the greatest of the Mughals—made

Babur is all ears to a shepherd on one of his journeys: scene from the Babur Nama.

between *dar-ul-sultanate* (the capital of the state) and *dar-ul-khalifa* (the seat of the emperor). Agra was never more than the capital by virtue of the emperor's presence. Yet in those one hundred years of being so honoured, Agra along with Cairo, Istanbul, Teheran and Peking, became one of the greatest cities of the east—the destination of

ambassadors, merchants, priests, artists and supplicants from the most distant corners of the known and civilised world, the seat of the Grand Mughal himself.

Shah Jahan, the richest and greatest of them all, lavished on it his masterpieces of Indo-Muslim architecture, none more entrancing than the jewelled tomb of his empress. Three hundred and fifty years later, at the end of the twentieth century, his requiem for Mumtaz Mahal remains one of the few real wonders wrought by the hand of man. Agra now belongs to the Taj Mahal.

FERMENT IN CENTRAL ASIA

It is only with the advent of Babur, the enterprising young Turk who forced his way into India in 1525, that Agra really came into its own. Born in 1483 in Farghana, a small principality to the north of the Hindu Kush mountains, Zahir-al-din Babur had waged a long and lonely battle to establish himself. Buffeted for years by Shaibani Khan, the Uzbek ruler, Babur managed to wrest for himself a small kingdom out of Kabul, Kandahar and Badakhshan, but not for long. Unable to withstand the hostility of his more powerful neighbours, Babur began to inch towards India, and the vacuum created by the death of the powerful Sikander Lodi aided him.

In 1525 Babur wrested a decisive victory from Ibrahim Lodi, Sikander's successor, annexing Punjab. Years later Babur would record in his memoirs: 'By God's mercy and kindness, this difficult affair was made easy for us! In one half day that armed mass was laid upon the earth. Five or six thousand men were killed in one place close to Ibrahim. Our estimate of the other dead, lying all over the field, was 15 to 16,000 but it came to be known later in Agra from the statements of Hindustanis, that 40 or 50,000 may have died in that battle.'

Soon, Babur had taken Delhi and Agra

and in keeping with tradition the *khutbah* (prayer for the ruler) was recited in Delhi. The newly proclaimed ruler of Hindustan galloped on to Agra where his son, Muhammad Humayun, had already taken possession of Sultan Ibrahim Lodi's fabulous treasure. The family of Raja Bikramjit of Gwalior, who was killed at Panipat, gave Humayun 'a mass of jewels . . . amongst which was the famous diamond', the Koh-i-noor (Mountain of Light). It remained with the House of Timur until Nadir Shah took it away to Persia after he sacked Delhi in 1739. Eventually it fell into the hands of Maharaja Ranjit Singh of the Punjab, but when the British annexed the province they sent the diamond to Queen Victoria and it has remained among the Crown jewels ever since.

Babur followed up his victory by making lavish gifts from the captured treasure to his followers, relations and friends in Afghanistan and Central Asia. His *begs* (generals), however, were not reconciled to the prospect of staying on in the intense heat of Hindustan. Babur himself found little to recommend it and was in two minds about settling here. However, he was put on his mettle by the much more serious threat of the Rajput confederacy under the renowned Rana Sanga of Mewar.

Once again Babur roused his followers to battle. As many as 2,01,000 men faced his minuscule army at Kanwaha near Fatehpur Sikri, but the strategy that had given him victory at Panipat succeeded again. Their foes 'dispersed like carded wool before the wind, and like moths scattered abroad'. The day ended with a characteristic Mongol-Turki victory celebration. 'Mounds were made of the bodies slain, pillars of their heads.' As for Babur, 'Thanks be to God!' he exclaimed; 'a Ghazi (killer of infidels) I became!' He was now committed to his kingdom in Hindustan, though he remained a Central Asian at heart and decreed that when he

died his body should be buried in the garden he had made in Kabul.

As it happened that day was to arrive much sooner than anyone thought. In 1530 his son Humayun fell seriously ill. As a last resort a well-known saint suggested that the emperor should make an offering of great value. Declaring that nothing could be more precious than his life, Babur circled

Humayun's bed thrice, praying: 'O God! If a life may be exchanged for a life, I, who am Babur, give my life and my being for Humayun.'

According to Babur's daughter Gulbadan, Babur was taken by fever the same day while Humayun, pouring water on his head, came out and gave audience. Babur never

Turkish dancers performing before Babur: scene from the Babur Nama.

recovered and died after a few months on 25 December 1530. Four days later the *khutbah* was read in Humayun's name. It was the first Mughal succession in Agra and the only one destined to be peaceful and undisputed.

Despite the unsettled life he was forced to

The obverse and reverse side, the former in 'kundan', the latter in 'meenakari' or enamelwork, of a Mughal ornament worn by women on their forehead.

lead from the day he became the ruler of Farghana, Babur was heir to the Persianised learning and cultural life of the capitals of the Turkish kingdoms in the valley of the Oxus. Two of his ancestors, Timur and Ulugh Beg, adorned Samarqand with

mosques, tombs, *madrassas* (schools) and *khanqas* (hospices), many of which still bear witness to the fifteenth-century Central Asian renaissance. In his memoirs Babur recalls that 'many stone-cutters brought from Hindustan' by Timur after his invasion had worked on the great Friday mosque. This was clear evidence of the interdependence of architecture and decoration more than a hundred years before Babur set foot in India.

Babur himself is the surest guide on this journey into the past. The *Babur Nama*, his memoirs written in the heat and passion of daily life, are the truest mirror of the times. They reveal him as a master of refined Turkish prose with a keen eye for the beauties of nature and a consuming passion for living life to the full. 'The flavour of the wine the drinker knows; what chance have sober men to know it?'

He scoured the hills surrounding Kabul for varieties of tulips and the flaming *arghwan* (Judas tree). 'If, the world over, there is a place to match this when the *arghwans* are in full bloom, I do not know it.' 'Tulips of many colours cover these foothills; I once counted . . . 32 or 33 different sorts. We named one the rose-scented . . . it grows by itself on Dast-i-Shaikh, here and nowhere else.'

Expressive lines of verse sprang quite naturally to his pen:

My heart, like the bud of the red, red rose,
Lies fold within fold aflame;
Would the breath of even a myriad springs,
Blow my heart's bud to a rose.

In more pensive mood, 'maddened and afflicted' for a boy in the camp bazaar when he was 17:

Nor power to go was mine, nor power to stay,
I was just what you made me, O thief of my heart.

Unhappily the surviving Turki text of

Babur's memoirs covers only 18 of the 47 years of his tumultuous life. In 1589, Babur's grandson Akbar directed his great general and statesman Abdur Rahim to translate the *Babur Nama* into Persian. Artists of the imperial atelier were commissioned to illustrate it with priceless miniatures, of which many have survived in the copy preserved at the National Museum in Delhi. Thus literature and art were fused with an excellence worthy of the peak of the Mughal age.

To Agra, and to Hindustan generally, Babur remained unreconciled to the end. 'It is a country of few charms', he laments. 'Its people have no good looks; of social intercourse, paying and receiving visits there is none; of manners none.'

His diatribe against Hindustan testifies more to the nostalgia of a man missing his homeland rather than to an inability to appreciate difference: 'There are no good horses, no good dogs, no grapes, musk melons or first rate fruits, no ice or cold water, no good bread or cooked food in the bazaars, no hot baths, no colleges, no candles, torches or candlesticks.' He acutely missed the familiar sounds of Central Asian life, and especially its gardens and streams running down from the hills.

One of the first things he did in Agra was to lay two gardens across the river. His *begs* followed the emperor's lead. 'The people of Hind', he says, 'who had never seen grounds planned so symmetrically and thus laid out, called the bank of the Jun (river Yamuna) where (our) residences were, Kabul.' One of these two gardens has survived, now known as Aram Bagh. Other gardens were laid at Dholpur and Sikri.

Babur's love of gardens was not just the aesthetic pose of a Central Asian longing for the delights of his homeland, but a necessary condition of life for him where the mind could be refreshed and the spirit revitalised.

HUMAYUN – A COMEDY OF ERRORS

The son for whom Babur gave his life was bereft of kingly attributes. Dominated by the senior ladies of the palace — his mother, Maham Begum, and sister, Gulbadan — his

A buckle has an emerald in the centre flanked by rubies and surrounded by diamonds.

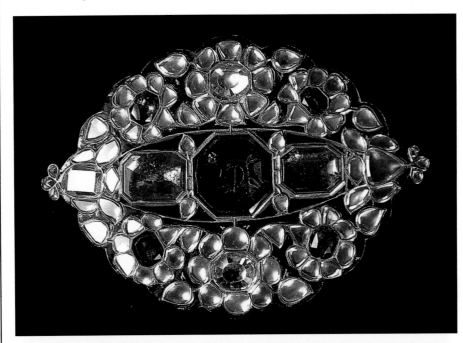

early promise in the field under his father evaporated when forced to fend for himself. The conquests left to his care were soon exposed to a looming threat from Sher Khan, an Afghan soldier who had carved out an estate for himself in Bihar. The

Overleaf : An aerial view of Agra Fort. In the forefront is the garden of Khas Mahal with the palace flanked by the cupolas of Samman Burj and Angoori Bagh.

23

جلال الدين اكبر بادشاه نشر

The Power and The Glory

Humayun nearly lost the kingdom Babur founded, but Akbar gave it root and sustenance,
the dynasty now springing from the soil of the land. His successors, Jahangir and Shah Jahan,
were aesthetes whose lasting contribution was in the field of refinement of arts and architecture.
Decline for the Mughal dynasty set in with Aurangzeb's ascendancy to the throne.

VERY EARLY in his long reign of 49 years, Akbar gave convincing proof of his outstanding qualities as a military leader, as a liberal patron of art and learning and as a creator of institutions of government, some of which persisted right up to Indian independence in 1947. This is all the more remarkable because when he ascended the throne at the age of 13 he was totally illiterate. So unsettled was his early life and so headstrong his character that he never learned to read and write, though he had a prodigious memory and a great deal of interest in books and mystical poetry. Akbar was also immensely strong and had a pronounced will of his own. Within four

years he had outgrown the overbearing influence of his old nurse and his faithful general Bairam Khan. By 1652 he was master in his own house. Thereafter he lost no time in laying down the policy of reconciliation and tolerance which was to distinguish his reign to the end.

With a perception amazing for a man who till then had no experience of government, Akbar realised that the extension and peace of his dominions would be a mirage unless it was sealed by political conciliation. The great princely states of Rajputana could imperil his base should he venture into the heartland of Hindustan. Defeating them in the field would have created sullen allies;

Facing page : Emperor Akbar was without doubt the Grand Mughal, for his rule witnessed the spread of his empire, alliances that gained him Rajput loyalty, and the first flourish of art that was to gain currency under his successors. Above : The 'sarpech' or ornament worn on a man's turban.

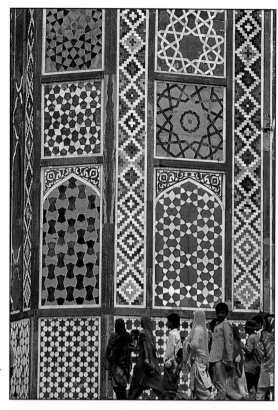

Right and below: Details from Sikandara, Akbar's tomb. The work on the walls show the pristine craftsmanship that marked many of the buildings of Akbar's era.

Jaisalmer and Dungarpur. Only the Sisodias of Mewar held aloof and, tragically, Rani Durgawati of Gondwana stabbed herself rather than give her hand.

CONQUEST

With the loyalty of most of the Rajput states assured, Akbar set himself a hectic pace of conquest. A rebellion in Gujarat on the western seaboard gave him an opportunity to prove his personal mettle. Mounted on swift camels, he arrived with a small force at the gates of Ahmedabad, covering 730 kilometres in nine days. He charged straight at the enemy as cries of 'Allah-hu Akbar' (God is great) and 'Ya Muin' (the name of a revered saint) rent the air. The rebellion was crushed. The fame of this exploit electrified Hindustan and was still being extolled 50 years later when foreign travellers were a common sight at his son's court.

With the conquest of Kashmir in 1586, the whole of the north from Kabul to as far south as Khandesh, and from Gujarat in the west to Bengal in the east, had been incorporated into Akbar's empire. Sind and Orissa were added in 1593. Only the states of the Deccan were left. When the emperor himself took command, Ahmednagar fell in 1600 and Asirgarh a few months later. At this point the campaign had to be called off because his son Salim's incipient rebellion demanded Akbar's presence in Agra.

Overshadowed by a brilliant and powerful father, Salim, who was later to become famous as Jahangir or 'World Seizer', revolted against Akbar seizing Allahabad, along with the revenues of Bihar, in 1601. Though galled, Akbar forgave him adding Bengal and Orissa to his governance. In 1602, however, when Salim struck coins in his own name, Akbar could tolerate his insubordination no more and sent a force to capture him which did not succeed. Finally in 1604, Akbar managed to subdue Salim and keep him to

winning them over was far more important. Breaking with all Muslim tradition, he sought and won the hand of the eldest daughter of Raja Bhara Mal of Amber (Jaipur) in the very year that he broke with his childhood mentors. The marriage won him the support of a powerful Rajput family; it was a development without parallel in any contemporary political order. Marriages were also arranged with princesses from Bikaner, his assigned quarters in Agra, till his own death in 1605.

CONCILIATION

Akbar's marriages to Rajput princesses was the clearest possible declaration of his policy of conciliation. Discriminatory taxes on non-Muslims, a common feature of Arab states and the Ottoman empire, had for centuries hurt the sensibilities of Indians in their own country, apart from being very irksome. In 1563 Akbar abolished the vexatious tax on pilgrims visiting Hindu holy places, and followed it up the very next year by doing away with the *jizya*, the hated poll tax on non-Muslims. For a young emperor still finding his way these measures called for exceptional self-confidence. Binyon has rightly described them as an assertion of Akbar's will and conscience against a tradition sanctioned by centuries of custom.

The most ambitious of the young emperor's attempts to break away from the confining effects of rigid orthodoxy was the creation of an over-arching religious order in which, in the words of his son Jahangir, 'the road to altercation would be closed'. After Akbar moved his court to Fatehpur Sikri in 1571, the great question on which he initiated debate was: 'If some true knowledge was . . . everywhere to be found, why should truth be confined to one religion?' He went on to enunciate the principle of Sulh-i-Kul, or 'universal concord'. It was a courageous attempt to establish a reign of tolerance as the religious counterpart of the political unity of his varied dominions.

Though he had a deep sense of the divine and was capable of genuine mystical experiences himself, Akbar's approach to religion was that of an astute statesman. In an attempt to unite the vastly varied faiths and divergent sects of his people, he devised an eclectic religious order called the Din-i-Ilahi or 'divine faith'. A controversial religious

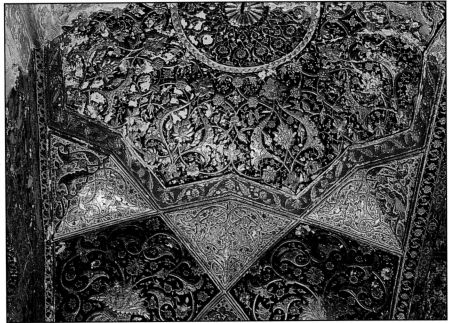

Left and below: Details from a painted wall and a ceiling in Akbar's tomb, Sikandara. A very fine quality of work distinguishes this seventeenth century mausoleum which is vastly different from the dome-enclosed cenotaphs of his father Humayun (in Delhi) or that built by his grandson Shah Jahan for his empress.

scheme, it conferred the supreme authority to decide all religious disputes on the emperor. An attempt was also made to surmount religious differences by drawing people together in personal allegiance to the emperor. However, it was difficult to shake the moorings of the orthodox and Akbar's 'divine faith' floundered due to lack of adherents. Akbar himself abandoned belief in his religion many years before his death.

INSTITUTIONS OF GOVERNMENT

What proved much more enduring were Akbar's administrative institutions. Only a highly centralised system could hold together his far-flung and highly diverse empire. The entire country was carved into *subas* (provinces), 15 to start with and then 21. As far as possible these replicated the older territorial divisions of states and provinces, which in turn incorporated the earlier revenue units or *parganas*. The emperor made all the governors as well as the officials (*mansabdars*) responsible for the collection of revenue in groups of *parganas*. An enormous army of petty officials prepared land records, classified land, assessed and collected the revenue in cash or kind and paid the proceeds into the *pargana tehsils*. The system was deceptively well ordered and perhaps unavoidable at the time. But since the *mansabs* were not hereditary, the holders of this office had little interest in anything more than squeezing the ryots. Correspondingly the ryots had no incentive to improve their holdings when the only prospect was of being relieved of more if they produced more. Unquestionably, the *mansabdari* system led to mass rural poverty when Akbar's strong hand was no longer there to control it.

The *mansabdars* were required to raise a stipulated number of troopers, and their horses were branded. Very soon, however, *mansabdari* became largely a ranking system. *Mansabs* of 5,000 became quite common, but the horses were openly recycled and were mostly pathetically unfit for warfare. The whole thing degenerated into an incubus. The land revenue system, on the other hand, endured. Its main features were adopted by the British and even later, in independent India, with necessary changes being made to provide security of occupancy rights and ownership. Raja Todar Mal is generally credited with being the originator of Akbar's

revenue system. For some time he had also worked for Sher Shah Suri, who must therefore be entitled to a share of the credit.

AKBAR'S COURT

When he first transferred his court to Agra in 1558, Akbar gave himself over to manly pursuits such as hunting, playing polo on

Facing page and below : Sikandara, Emperor Akbar's final resting place, was begun in his lifetime as an open pyramidal tomb and was of red sandstone. It was completed after his death by Jahangir who provided it with a highly decorative gate, enclosing the tomb within a large garden; the tomb itself he topped with marble, the cloistered pavilion being left open in compliance with his father's wishes.

the grounds outside the old Badalgarh Fort and riding elephants. By the time he was 16 he learnt to dominate even *mast* elephants, a hazardous sport he favoured for many years thereafter. His son Jahangir records that he was often seen to leap on the backs of these dangerous animals from a wall or overhanging branch and subdue them. One of his most stirring encounters was seen by thousands of his amazed subjects when he mounted Hawai ('like the wind'), which had been Hemu's elephant at the battle of Panipat in 1556, and gave chase to Ranbagha, a beast nearly as formidable. Ranbagha turned tail and fled, with Akbar in full chase, over

Amar Singh Gate, one of the principal entrances to Agra Fort, so named to commemorate the escape on horseback from its ramparts of a Rajput foe who won Akbar's admiration for this act of daring: imminent battle

animals. When he was just 19, and returning from the conquest of Malwa, he attacked a tigress with five cubs near the fort of Narwar. 'His Majesty', says Abu'l-Fazl, 'with swift foot and alert arm attacked the brute and killed it with one stroke of his sword.' Allowing for a courtier's fulsome flattery, there is little doubt that Akbar was a man of reckless courage. And as for his strength, he could run along the battlements of Agra Fort with a man under each arm, and he once walked about 48 kilometres from Mathura to Agra at such a pace that only three of his followers could keep up with him.

In 1565, though only 23, he had achieved enough to stimulate ideas of imperial grandeur. 'Accordingly', says his biographer Abu'l-Fazl, 'he at this time gave directions for the building in Agra—*which by its position is the centre of Hindustan*—of a grand fortress such as might be worthy thereof, and correspond to the dignity of his dominions.' Unquestionably the Agra Fort is the finest of its kind from Attock in the north to Allahabad at the confluence of the rivers Ganga and Yamuna.

The fort was ready in eight years, but the Rajput queen from Amber was able to occupy Bengali Mahal in 1569. However, the court was not destined to stay in Agra much longer. None of the children born to the queen had survived. Greatly troubled, Akbar sought the intercession of the saint of Sikri, Sheikh Salim Chishti, who had sent him away with a promise of not one but three sons. When the Rajput queen became enceinte, a small palace was made for her close to the saint's hermitage. In due time a prince was born who was named Salim after the saint. Murad and Daniyal were born to other ladies of the harem, making sure of the succession.

Two years later, in 1571, the emperor's gratitude to the saint was expressed by the creation of a capital on Sikri hill, renamed Fatehpur after his victory in Gujarat. Agra

or aggression, or a falling out from imperial favour, would result in the closure of the gates, making the citadel impregnable.

the bridge of boats. It was a miracle that the bridge did not collapse. There is a striking miniature of this dramatic episode in the *Akbar Nama.*

Akbar's love of danger lured him into numerous hair-raising encounters with wild may have lost much of its glamour when the emperor took his court away, but it was never abandoned. The treasure and much else must have remained in the great fort. Ralph Fitch, an early British trader, visited the capital in the summer of 1585. 'Agra and Fatehpur,' he says, 'are two very great cities, either of them much greater than London and very populous.' All the way between 'is a market of victuals and other things, as full as though a man were still in a town, and so many people as if a man were in a market!' Fatehpur was indeed the cultural and administrative twin of Agra. But whether at Lahore or anywhere else, the imperial camp was always the capital. This was a relic from the nomadic Turko-Mongol past. Wherever he was, in the grandeur of Agra Fort or on the march by horse or camel, or even as a pilgrim journeying on foot to Hazrat Ajmer, or yet again with splendid equipage on the great northern road planned and surveyed by his grandfather, the imperial capital was his camp, moving with him wherever he went.

According to the Jesuit Monserrate, who joined in vigorous debate with the *ulema* at Fatehpur, work on the new capital was still going on. Akbar threw himself into the project with his customary energy, often working alongside the builders. There is a fascinating miniature in the *Akbar Nama* which shows the emperor supervising construction. Fourteen years after he moved to Fatehpur, Dar-ul-Khilafat went to the north, taking root in Lahore. An insurrection in Kabul had to be dealt with, Kashmir conquered and Sind added to the empire. Attempts have been made to suggest natural and even mystical reasons for the emperor's departure from Fatehpur. The commonest explanation is said to be shortage of water, but it could not have been as scarce then as it is now. The Sikri lake was full, the wells well stocked, so much so that the main water lift worked the cooling system in the palace

and sent water flowing down the channels of the imperial complex on the hill.

It has also been suggested that the emperor's eclecticism, verging on heresy, which took final form in a declaration of his infallibility in 1579, caused deep distress to the saint of Sikri. A sense of regret is thought

Within Agra Fort, all but the emperor and the princes had to dismount and walk; the royal family's arrivals and departures were announced by heralds.

to have induced Akbar to leave the place in peace after the great religious debates of that decade. Considering that the saint died in 1572, even this suggestion lacks plausibility. William Finch, who visited Fatehpur in 1610 while on the way to buy indigo in Bayana,

Overleaf : The arches and colonnades of the Diwan-i-Am at Agra Fort where the emperor would meet with senior officials and select guests for private meetings.

picked up an even more lurid story. 'Under the courtyard (of the mosque) is a goodly tank of excellent water; none other being to be had through the cities, but brackish and fretting, by drinking whereof was caused such mortality that the Acubar, before it was quite finished left it, and removed his seat to Agra; so that this goodlie citie was short-lived, in fifty or sixty years space being built and ruinate.' I deliberately drank the water of all the wells in Fatehpur, in the old town of Sikri and the neighbourhood, only to find that this story about the water being 'brackish and fretting' was a latter-day invention. In fact water in the whole of Braj, and this includes Mathura and Agra as well, is slightly saline.

Wherever Akbar went in the empire, the inner chambers of the palace were guarded by Tartar women warriors armed with bows and arrows and short daggers, while, as Abu'l-Fazl says, 'at a proper distance there is

a guard of faithful Rajputs'. It is a tribute to Akbar's policy of reconciliation that the men who had held out against the emperor at Chittor and Ranthambhor before throwing themselves at the siege-guns were the very ones to whose courage and loyalty Akbar entrusted the security of his own person.

Apart from the distinctive Mughal institutes of government, it was during the momentous years at Fatehpur that Akbar developed an elaborate court ceremonial inspired by the concept of his semi-divinity. Much of it was influenced by Jain and Parsi rites. Two Jesuits who arrived there before Akbar left for the north convinced themselves that he was well on the way to accepting Christianity. They were profoundly dejected when he showed interest in other religions as well. An open minded eclectic can be claimed by adherents of most religions, but there is considerable evidence of Akbar being deeply interested in Hindu mysticism. He often communed with

Facing page and above: Akbar's Diwan-i-Khas or hall of private audience at Fatehpur Sikri is vastly different from that in Agra. It was atop this capital that the emperor would seat himself; he could be approached only by very senior ministers from the walkways angling out in all directions (they in turn would be seated in the balconies surrounding the column). It is not difficult to imagine him suspended in mid-air as it were, while around him his chosen few, the 'nine jewels' with whom he liked to surround himself, engaged the emperor in conversation.

a renowned mystic in Mathura, and in his court ceremonial borrowed freely from Hindu and Parsi practices to create a ritual of his own to go with his new faith. Even a large lantern suspended from a great height in front of the Diwan-i-Am in Fatehpur was called *akash diya*, a purely Hindi term meaning sky lamp.

A largely festive occasion was the monthly

Entrance to the cenotaph chamber of Itmad-ud-Daulah. Pietra-dura inlay was used brilliantly for the first time in this mausoleum. The Rajput palaces were fond of painting all available spaces; the

Mughals by now fancied more lavish decoration, and inlay in their stone buildings gave them an adornment which Hindustan had earlier reserved only for its jewellery.

khushroz (day of rejoicing) when high-born ladies displayed choice articles of handiwork and their own charms. It became a recognized marriage market at which aspiring beauties hoped to catch the emperor's eye. Akbar's harem had no less than 5,000 young women. Akbar's son Prince Salim was ensnared by a dazzling Persian beauty at just

such a meena bazaar. After his accession she made a place for herself in history as the domineering Empress Nur Jahan.

The women of the harem were not queens, some of whom had apartments in the palace. They were largely entertainers, trained to sing and dance. Some of them excelled in other arts. François Bernier, a clinically observant French doctor in the service of a senior nobleman, was extravagant in his praise: 'Most of these *kanchanis* are handsome and well dressed and sing to perfection; and their limbs being extremely supple, they dance with wonderful agility, and are always correct in regard to time.' Bernard, a Frenchman at Jahangir's court, was so taken by a *kanchani* that he importuned the emperor for her hand. A delighted Jahangir readily granted his wish and he carried his lady love away on his shoulders. At the time British visitors to the court were a severe lot, dedicated to trade and making money. They seem to have been totally unresponsive to the charms of the women of the harem.

On his arrival in Agra Akbar sent an invitation to Tan Sen, the greatest singer of the age, who was then at the court of the ruler of Gwalior. His compositions ran into thousands, and his voice melted the hearts of his listeners. Even earlier, Akbar's grisly old Turkish general Bairam Khan had been reduced to tears by the singing of Ram Das. At this time the Mughal court was instrumental in ensuring the survival and propagation of the two traditional Indian art forms of music and dance.

What proved most enduring of all was the art of painting. It started with a commission given by Humayun to Mir Sayyid Ali and Khwaja Abdus Samad of Tabrez while he was still in Kabul, to paint more than a thousand folios illustrating the Persian epic *Dastan-i-Amir Hamzah*. Akbar extended his patronage to them on the death of his father, and recruited artists from all over northern India to the atelier he set up in Agra and subsequently in Fatehpur.

At its peak there were over a hundred artists in the imperial *karkhanah*, many more Indians than Persians and Central Asians. While techniques and artistic sensibility are quite easily detectable as separate strands, both tended to merge into a common style under Akbar's personal inspiration. Abu'l-Fazl was constrained to allow that 'whilst the number of those who approach perfection . . . is very large, this is especially true of the Hindus; their pictures surpass our perception of things'. Basawan, Sanwal Das, Tara Chand and Jagannath became household names in those far off days. The catholicity of Akbar's taste is revealed by the commissions he gave to the *karkhanah*: the *Chingiz Nama*, *Zafar Nama* (History of the House of Timur), his own *Akbar Nama*, and classical Sanskrit works such as the *Ramayana* and *Mahabharata* which the emperor ordered to be translated into Persian. The miniatures in the *Babur Nama*, to any mind, are the most outstanding of all.

Jahangir continued the tradition established by his father. His main interest was in flowers, birds and animals. The work of his great master Mansur is distinguished by meticulous attention to detail, though without any loss of animation. The story is told that when Sir Thomas Roe was at Jahangir's court, his artists prepared so perfect a copy of a picture given to them by the English envoy that he could not make out the difference between the original and the copy. Shah Jahan's chief artist was the Indian Muslim Faqirullah Khan, and his son Dara Shikoh was a patron in the mystic genre. Aurangzeb's intolerant attitude to music and singing proved a discouragement to artists generally. Singers, musicians and artists looked for other patrons, and by doing so stimulated the birth of very lively local schools. In the world of miniature painting the most notable of these came to be in

Rajputana and the Himalayan hill states of Himachal.

JAHANGIR, SHAH JAHAN, AURANGZEB

The pageant of the Mughal capital at Agra had been brilliantly illuminated by Akbar. He returned to it from Lahore in 1598 to spend the last seven years of his life in the

The cenotaph chamber with its fretwork stone screen : for Ghiyas Beg who had to flee from high office in Persia and arrive penniless in India, his rise in the Mughal court was no less than meteoric, and as prime minister he carried out his duties with deserving honour. His widowed daughter married Jahangir to become the most powerful empress of the dynasty.

great fort, a rather disappointed and unhappy man. His generals failed him in the Deccan, but the most bitter blow was the rebellion of his son Salim. Akbar subdued his son, it is said, by a blow of his strong right arm. Yet when he died in 1605 he left a generally well ordered empire to his chastened son.

In an age of largely uninstitutionalised

government it was to be expected that the personality of the emperor would make an immediate difference. Akbar's three successors could not have been more different from him and also one from the other. Salim, a naturally indolent and peace-loving man with a remarkable appreciation of art, assumed the improbable title of Jahangir, or 'World Seizer'. His masterful wife, Nur Jahan, was the actual ruler in all but name. Her Persian father was appointed prime minister with the title of Itmad-ud-Daulah, while the daughter of her brother, Asaf Khan, was given in marriage to the third prince, Khurram. When Jahangir died in 1627, Asaf Khan helped his son-in-law to the throne through a sea of blood, and was rewarded by being made prime minister.

Amongst her many accomplishments, the chief of which was to beguile the emperor into submission, Nur Jahan was a brilliant shot with the gun. Near Mathura she once killed four tigers with six shots, all of which found their mark. Her doting husband declared that such shooting had never been seen, particularly from a howdah on the back of an elephant. To do him justice, Jahangir continued his father's policy of tolerance, perhaps more from indolence than conviction. Akbar had given the Jesuits permission to build a church in Agra, which was completed during Jahangir's reign. At Mumtaz Mahal's reputed instance, Shah Jahan had the bell tower torn down, but the original crypt is still in existence.

At no time during India's known history was such lavish display the leitmotif of imperial rule as during Shah Jahan's reign (1627-58). It was saved from purposeless vulgarity by the emperor's exquisite taste. More to the point, however, was a general institutional decline. The *mansabdari* system, which was the linchpin of the administration as devised by Akbar, rapidly went to seed. The number was greatly reduced so that the selected few could be awarded ranks aimed at status rather than function. Shah Jahan had a *mansab* of 30,000 before he seized the throne, and his son Dara Shikoh was honoured with one of 60,000. It was fast becoming meaningless.

Mughal ascendancy, which was Akbar's unique achievement, and two generally peaceful decades that followed under Jahangir, had left Shah Jahan with a treasury

Below : Empress Nur Jahan, who had coins struck in her name and jointly signed firmans with her husband, was known for her fine taste in jewellery. Facing page : Samples of Mughal jewellery dating from the 17th century onwards

brimming over. He was able to gratify his passion for building almost immediately after other aspirants to the throne were liquidated. The death in 1631 of his much loved wife and constant companion while he was at Burhanpur in the Deccan gave him an occasion to indulge his fondness for architecture by enshrining her mortal remains

include a necklace, ear-ring, and a 'tika' for the forehead as well as one worn on the side of the head; also included is a gold bangle and an anklet-band. Some of these pieces can be compared with those in the portrait above.

Preceding pages : The cenotaphs of Mumtaz Mahal (in the centre) and Shah Jahan (to its side) are enclosed by a screen that took ten years in the making, its fretted screens carved from complete blocks of marble and set in frames of

pietra dura inlay. The cenotaph of the empress has a slate on it, that of the emperor an inkwell.
Above and facing page :
Obverse and reverse of gold coins current in the Mughal era.

in the most beautiful mausoleum ever built.

Work started on the Taj Mahal in 1632 and continued until the entire complex was completed 22 years later. Shah Jahan had already left Agra, or Akbarabad as it had come to be popularly known, for the traditional capital of Delhi. He sailed down the river Yamuna to see the completed masterpiece. Work had continued in his absence, strictly according to the designs he had already approved. He had seen the main work through, and left the finishing touches to the Mimar-i-Kul (chief architect) and the teams of specialists engaged in inlay, Nastaliq lettering, polishing of marble and the like.

Shah Jahan was to return to the Jasmine Tower he had built in the fort, this time as a prisoner, with just enough sight in his eyes to gaze at his greatest creation downriver. After disposing of the liberal-minded scholar, Dara Shikoh, the emperor's eldest son, Aurangzeb, closed his heart to the call of mercy and in 1658 locked up his own father in a marble prison. There he remained with only his devoted daughter to care for him, till he died in 1666.

The usurper Aurangzeb preferred the traditional capital of Delhi to the place where his father was imprisoned, thus bringing down the curtain on the heydays of Agra.

THE MUGHAL COURT

Under the Mughals, Agra became the seat of the greatest empire seen in Hindustan for a thousand years, a kaleidoscope of colour and brilliant spectacle. At the centre of it all was the emperor himself, and no one more outstanding than Akbar who was pre-eminently the creator. Seated in the Diwan-i-Am of his massive new Agra Fort, here was all the power and glory of the Mughal empire. For here was the Shahinshah (king of kings), the embodiment of all authority in matters of state. With the issue of the *Mazhar Nama* (Declaration) in 1579, he became also the Imam of the Age. The Shahinshah was thus the viceregent of God, clothed with temporal and spiritual authority undreamt of in the contemporary world.

In the Diwan-i-Am, or hall of public audience, says Abu'l-Fazl, 'he is visible . . . to people of all ranks . . . without any molestation from the mace-bearers. This mode of showing himself is called, in the language of the country, *darshan*.' It was an old Hindu custom which was adopted by Akbar as a living compact with the people of his empire. When he saluted the morning sun, Akbar was visible to people who had collected in the street below; but the first formal *darshan* was after the first watch, about nine o'clock, when he appeared in the *jharoka* (audience balcony) facing the Diwan-i-Am, crowded with high nobles and supplicants. A further audience was sometimes arranged later in the evening. Not even personal tragedy prevented Akbar from performing his part. The very next day after his mother's death he sat in the *jharoka* and ordered the celebration of Dussehra, the principal Hindu festival, with due ceremony.

Protocol inside the palace was regulated to the minutest detail. Three forms of salutation were prescribed—the *kornish*, *tasleem* and finally *sijda* or prostration. Shah Jahan did away with *sijda*. Jahangir made the picturesque addition of the chain of justice. It was made of four *maunds* of pure gold and strung with 60 bells. Secured to a post in the street below, a supplicant could attract the emperor's attention by giving it a tug.

The ceremonial with which Akbar surrounded himself had the central purpose of making himself accessible. Justice and public audience were his two principal instruments for satisfying the expectations of his people, and he arranged his daily programme so that he could regularly perform the duties of a sovereign. Wherever he went he was surrounded by crowds.

The plan of the great fort, and subsequently of the imperial complex in Fatehpur, provided for the emperor's public functions. The palaces he built in Agra Fort were demolished by his son and grandson so that they could indulge their fancy for florid opulence. However, the Akbari design has been preserved in Fatehpur, in which his heirs showed no interest. In keeping with his compact with the people, the focal point is the Diwan-i-Am, and beyond it, in the direction of Sheikh Salim Chishti's tomb, a large courtyard surrounded mostly by functional buildings, some of great beauty.

Further in came the Daulat Khana or imperial residence with palaces of favoured queens close by. No one could enter the Daulat Khana without a summons from the emperor himself. As in Agra, Akbar made an appearance at a *jharoka* in the southern wall of the Diwankhana-i-Khas below his

Overleaf: Entrance to the crypt-rooms of Sikandara, representative of Akbar's eclectic taste in architecture, art and religion.

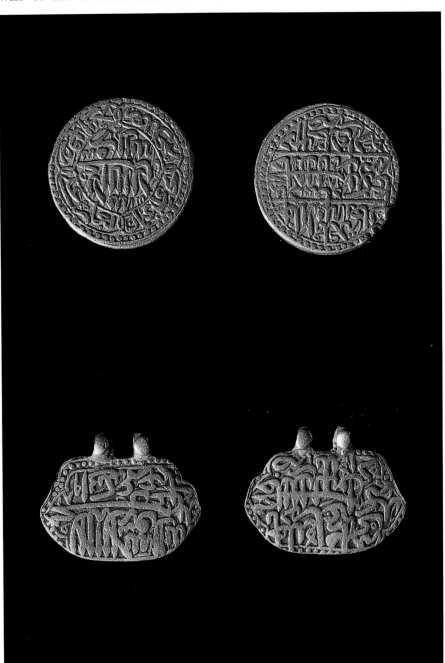

khwabgah or sleeping chamber for his first informal *darshan* of the day. At about nine o' clock he seated himself in the Diwan-i-Am directly facing the public.

Akbar's popularity was unbounded, but even he insisted on the usual symbols of

authority, one of which was the throne. It was to be expected, however, that Shah Jahan's unrestrained passion for magnificence would be expressed by the commissioning of a throne of unsurpassed beauty. This was the so-called Peacock Throne. It took seven years to make, and Shah Jahan was able to sit on it on Id-ul-Fitr of 1634-5. The French jeweller Tavernier was able to examine it

shaped pearl of 50 carats or thereabouts'. Tavernier counted as many as 108 of the finest rubies, some of 200 carats or more, and 116 emeralds. In his opinion, 'the most costly point about this magnificent throne is that the twelve columns supporting the canopy are surrounded by beautiful rows of pearls, which are round and of fine water'.

Alas for posterity, when Nadir Shah of Persia sacked Delhi in 1739 the Peacock Throne was his most prized trophy. It was subsequently broken up and became a memory even before the extinction of the House of Timur.

CITY OF SPECTACLES

One of Akbar's innovations was the revival of the old Hindu custom of the sovereign's ceremonial weighing against articles of value. What made it specially noteworthy was that the ceremony was observed by a Muslim ruler of a dynasty only recently arrived in Hindustan. Akbar was ceremonially weighed twice a year, on both his solar and lunar birthdays. On the solar birthday he was weighed against 12 articles including gold, mercury, silk, perfumes and other costly items. The lunar birthday weighing was against eight articles of which silver and tin were the most expensive. The value of the articles weighed was later distributed to mendicants and the poor crowding the palace. The emperor's birthday was also keenly awaited: it was the day when promotions and rewards were announced and costly gifts presented.

The most colourful of the festivals celebrated by Akbar was the old Parsi feast of *Nauroz* or the New Year. It commenced when the sun moved into Aries and lasted 19 days. Banquets were the order of the day, along with music and singing. Several of the celebrations observed by Akbar had a mystical significance. He believed that fire and light were manifestations of the divine.

closely when the court shifted to Delhi. The throne itself was solid gold, covered by a canopy studded with gems and set off by a string of pearls. On top was 'a peacock with (an) elevated tail made of blue sapphires and other coloured stones, the body of gold with inlaid precious stones, having a large ruby in front of the breast, whence hangs a pear-

Every year, at noon of the day when the sun entered the nineteenth degree of Aries, a fire was lit by exposing a *surajkarant* (a convex crystal acting like a magnifying glass). The fire was carefully tended the whole year until it was time for renewal.

Another eagerly awaited occasion was *khushroz* in the meena bazaar, described earlier, but in 1632 and 1633 Peter Mundy witnessed celebrations the like of which he could never have imagined. This mercurial Cornishman spent some years at the English factory in Agra, revelling in the excitement of life in the city during Shah Jahan's reign. On 1 June 1632, he recounts in his *Relations* the celebrations marking Shah Jahan's return from the Deccan. Mingling with the throng he saw columns of camels, elephants with howdahs, and thousands of horsemen with long lances glittering in the sun as they careered over the plain. 'All the face of the earth, soe far as wee could see, was covered with people, troopes of horse, eliphants etts, with innumerable flags small and greate, which made a most gallant show.' There were 20 coaches for the emperor, who followed on a dark grey horse flanked by the highest amirs and prince Dara Shikoh, his favourite. 'All these moving in on one, on so many huge elephants, seemed like a fleet of ships with flags and streamers . . . so that all these together made a most majestical, war-like and delightsome sight.'

Mundy made some pen-and-ink sketches of these unusual sights, but his skill seems to have been unequal to the breathtaking display of fireworks in February of the following year to celebrate the marriages of the princes Dara Shikoh and Shuja. A myriad oil lamps and other illuminations decorated the walls, palaces and pavilions all the way to the top. Then there was a deafening explosion of firecrackers. Mundy describes 'great elephants whose bellies were full of squibs, crackers, etc.; giants with wheels in their hands, then a rank of

monsters, then of turrets, then of artificial trees, (and other) inventions, all full of rockets, etc. . . . All these being fired, although not at one time, innumerable were the rockets, reports, squibs and crackers that flew about and aloft in the air, making the night like day.'

Shah Jahan squandered the empire's wealth, but he left for posterity the Taj Mahal

and the palaces in Agra Fort. For what should he be remembered—for subordinating his grandfather's institutes of government to his passion for opulence, or as the creator of the finest monuments of the age, or yet again as the bloodthirsty murderer of his brothers?

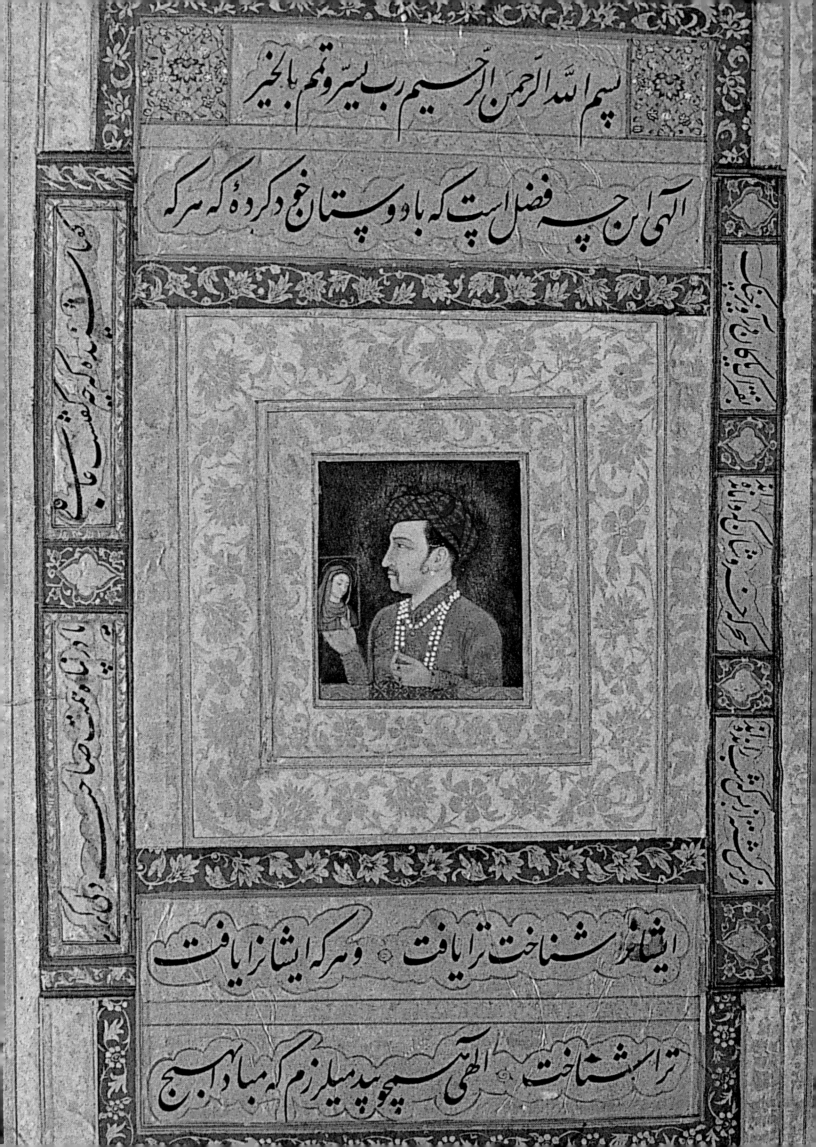

بسم الله الرحمن الرحيم رب يسّر وتمّم بالخير

الهی این چه فضل است که با دوستان خود کرده که هر که

ایشان را شناخت ترا یافت · و هر که ایشان را یافت

ترا شناخت الهی سپید میلزم که مباد که

Agra's Glorious Architecture

Babur had little time between his campaigns to concentrate on building, though he
introduced the formal Persian garden to Indian soil. Akbar's architectural heritage is Fatehpur Sikri,
a city planned on a grand scale, though it was soon abandoned. Jahangir's impressions are to be
found in the palaces within Agra Fort, and in the cenotaphs commemorating his father
and father-in-law. But it was Shah Jahan who was the biggest builder of them all.

*E*mperors turn to dust just as surely as
ordinary mortals; their works dwindle to
short paragraphs of history, but the Mughal
legend still survives mainly on the strength
of their architectural creations. Most of the
Mughals were great builders. Even Babur in
his brief reign of four years laid gardens
with pavilions and running water. His mood
was frankly nostalgic, seeking echoes of his
beloved Farghana and the harsher climes of
Afghanistan where he spent 20 years before
committing himself to the conquest of
Hindustan. Yet his garden in Agra and the
exiguous remains of a rather ambitious one
near Dholpur are proof enough that the

Turki genius for architecture was prevented
by premature death from finding more
abundant expression.

Humayun's contribution to Mughal
architecture is his very large red sandstone
tomb, with soft-stone inlays of marble. His
death being accidental, the tomb was built
by his widow with generous help from his
young successor, Akbar. Its main significance
is the double dome, first introduced in India
by the preceding Lodi dynasty. Set in a
spacious formal *charbagh* (subdivided squares)
with water channels, the tomb was boldly
innovative with its subtle interweaving of
Hindu and Islamic styles.

*Facing page : Emperor
Jahangir, the fourth Mughal to
occupy the throne of Hindustan,
was more an aesthete and a
connoisseur than a ruler, and it
became widely known that Nur
Jahan was the power behind the
throne while 'the king was such
only in name'. Above :
Diamonds are set into a gold
bracelet clasped by gilded chains
of the same precious metal.*

Top : The pristine Itmad-ud-Daulah is like a mosaic-decorated jewel casket. Its short minarets contribute to its elegance of form, for their height does not overshadow the low, square roof. The corner kiosks and eaves supported by brackets are an indication of how Indian architecture was employed in a Persian building with success.
Right : Details from the facade of Itmad-ud-Daulah with the bold inlay pattern standing out in relief. A distinctive feature of the mausoleum is the use of different colours of marble and jasper, and the designs are geometrical and floral patterns permitted by Islam.

AGRA FORT

The year 1565 marks the real birth of Mughal architecture in Agra and indeed in the whole of their empire. Akbar was just 23; he had already conquered Malwa, and, as his biographer Abu'l-Fazl writes, he decided that 'an impregnable fort should be built of hewn stones' that would be 'worthy of the dignity of his dominions'. Abu'l-Fazl

writes that the foundations were laid 'in an hour which was supreme for establishing a fortress'. According to tradition the participation in the ceremony of the Rajput raja of neighbouring Karauli was necessary to ensure that the fort would be protected from erosion by the rivers. Akbar was always punctilious in honouring local sentiment. The river has never endangered the fort's sheer walls.

Honouring Hindu sentiments was symbolic of Akbar's spirit of reconciliation, but the choice of hewn stones as the primary material of construction was a momentous decision. The easy availability of red sandstone from the quarries of Rajputana and of marble from Makrana not only helped Akbar switch over from using burnt bricks but also to embark on huge programmes of construction. It was a decision which enabled the Mughals to earn the well-deserved title of master builders.

There are definite indications that the old Rajput fort of Badalgarh was levelled and Akbar's fort built upon the site. Jahangir makes the categorical statement that his father 'threw down' the old fort, while Abu'l-Fazl further clarifies that: 'An inevitable mandate was issued that the old fort . . . should be removed, and in that place should be founded an impregnable palace.' Qasim Khan, the amir in charge of works, was thus able to take advantage of the height of the compacted debris of the old fort of Badalgarh to give Akbar's 'impregnable palace' its distinctive feature of a series of rising planes.

The great fort was completed in eight years, but the princess from Amber, Mariam Makani, was able to occupy Bengali Mahal four years later in 1569. Work must have proceeded at a furious pace, with the emperor, in his usual way, keeping architects and workmen on their toes. The stone slab facing of the masonry walls 'were so joined together', Abu'l-Fazl claims, 'that the end of a hair could not find a place between them'. The Jesuit Monserrate, who spent two years at Akbar's court from 1580, was equally enthusiastic. 'The stones of these building are so cunningly fitted that the joints are scarcely visible, although no lime was used to fix them together. The beautiful colour of the stone, which is all red, produces the same effect of uniform solidity.' That is the impression the visitor gets even today.

The fort was designed as a stronghold with underground vaults for the treasure, and also as a residence for the emperor, his senior wives, guards and prominent court officials. Akbar took advantage of this opportunity to give expression, in the lasting medium of stone, to his syncretic approach to the arts — taking the best from all traditions. According to Abu'l-Fazl, more than five hundred red sandstone buildings were erected in the fort, 'in the fine styles of Bengal and Gujarat'. He might have added the Tomar architecture of Gwalior to his list, for the interior of Jahangiri Mahal bears a striking resemblance to the Man Mandir Palace in Gwalior. Some of the reliefs in this palace are of the very highest quality and represent a break with the earlier Sultanate styles of decoration, mainly of carved stucco.

There was a similar outburst of building activity on both banks of the river by the leading amirs and courtiers. There are a few remains on the left bank; all else has disappeared. After the Revolt of 1857 the British, in a fit of pique or perhaps genuine apprehension, blew up the incomparably beautiful palace of Shah Jahan's father-in-law, Asaf Khan, and the mansions of several other nobles facing the cantonment and along the riverfront, allegedly to clear the glacis.

Similarly, the wholesale destruction of the five hundred or so Akbari buildings in the Bengal and Gujarat styles by his grandson Shah Jahan was an incalculable loss to Indo-

Top : Jahangiri Mahal, a red sandstone palace, is one of the few surviving buildings originally made by Akbar, and exhibits influences of Hindu architecture as seen at Gwalior's Man Mandir Palace. The facade is decorated with tiles with marble relief, and the square domed hall and grand central court are supposedly 'entirely Hindu in character'. Left : Brackets from an open hall in Jahangiri Mahal, again similar to those in Man Mandir, which have been described by Carleylle as 'cross-beams, which are ornamented with the quaint device of a great serpent or dragon carved on them lengthways... unique and without a parallel in its design'.

Muslim architecture. Of the buildings Akbar made hardly anything remains except Jahangiri Mahal, the Naqqar Khana (drum house over the entrance) and the ruined traces of Bengali Mahal and his own Akbari Mahal. Shah Jahan's partiality in favour of white marble instead of the soft tones of red sandstone was justified by his biographer, Mulla Abdul Lahori, by deceptively simple sophistry: 'By the command of His Majesty

Below : *Khas Mahal in Agra Fort, a dazzling marble pavilion fronting the river that was occupied by Princess Jahanara, with the recessed courtyard in front forming Angoori Bagh, the garden of grapes.*

Above : *Of the five hundred or so palaces and apartments that Akbar built within the fort, few have survived, among them the ruins of Machhi Bhawan.*

(Akbar) were built in that heaven-like fort lofty buildings of red sandstone for royal residence. As in this everlasting reign (Shah Jahan's) the demand for arts has a different market and the Divine care has adopted a new method of embellishing the world, at the place of the old have been built sky-touching mansions of marble.' Shah Jahan's paranoia deprived the Agra Fort of what could have become an unrivalled museum of architectural styles. Although of great beauty in themselves the marble palaces he built instead create an effect of over-abundance, with few soft-toned interiors such as were achieved in the traditional Hindu architecture of Jahangiri Mahal. Moreover, they must have needed a heavy padding of carpets to protect the inmates from the blinding glare of the Agra sun.

Making straight up the ramp to the Diwan-i-Am, as the leading amirs and courtiers did for the emperor's *darshan*, the walled courtyard and cloisters are all that remain of Akbar's original. A superbly proportioned *chaalis satun* (hall supported by forty pillars), finished with shell plaster, was reserved for the high-born who came to make the *taslim*. The Akbari sandstone *jharoka*, according to Mulla Abdul Hamid, was rebuilt by Shah Jahan in marble, inlaid with precious stones of various colours, 'and the ceiling embossed with gold and made a counterpart of the roof of heaven'.

Further east, and completely separated from the Diwan-i-Am, wonders follow in quick succession. Beyond the large courtyard of Machhi Bhawan is the beautifully proportioned double-pillared Diwan-i-Khas, or hall of private audience. A Persian inscription in Nastaliq characters in the south wall opens with the lines:

The erection of this delightful lofty palace Has exalted Akbarabad to the Arsh (ninth Heaven)

In the mid-eighteenth century the Jats of the neighbouring kingdom of Bharatpur looted the courtyard facing the Diwan-i-Khas and Machhi Bhawan of their finest marbles, sparing only the black marble throne hewn from a single slab. The credulous maintain that when it was mounted by the Jat ruler, it cracked from side to side and blood gushed out! The red discolouration is due to nothing more alarming than the presence of iron in the marble.

Unless it is pointed out, one is apt to miss a small *chhattri* as perfect as the dome of Brunelleschi's Pazzi chapel; along the southern wall of Machhi Bhawan, says Mulla Abdul Hamid, is 'an umbrella embossed pavilion of white marble on four pillars in extreme elaboration and purity. In this pavilion the golden throne, exalted like the seventh Heaven, is honoured by His Majesty's seat on it'. No more fitting place for the Peacock Throne can be imagined.

Behind the Diwan-i-Khas is the Daulatkhana-i-Khas, Shah Jahan's personal residence. It is unquestionably the finest royal apartment in India, with marble walls decorated by 'various paintings and adorned with gold'. The parlour with its sunk marble pool is unsurpassed for the refinement of its decoration. The Jasmine Tower rising out of the perimeter wall is where Shah Jahan, during his imprisonment, is said to have gazed at the image of the Taj in a mirror inlaid in one of its pillars.

Further south is the Khas Mahal where Jahanara Begum lived while she cared for her imprisoned father. The Hammam, or bath, was deprived of its best marbles which were sent to the Prince Regent, and is now closed. Sheesh Mahal, or the Palace of Mirrors, defies description. Mini waterfalls, lighted from within, produce effects in the mirrors that are totally enchanting.

Hidden away to the north-west of the Diwan-i-Khas is the finest gem of all, the Moti Masjid or Pearl Mosque. There is one in the Lahore Fort too, and one in Delhi, usually intended for the royal family and close attendants. For purity of form the Agra Pearl Mosque has no equal anywhere. One of the lines inscribed in the entablature over the front row of pillars compares Akbar's fort with 'a halo round the shining moon'.

The visitor enters a totally different world in Jahangiri Mahal. It is built entirely of lustrous red sandstone with some marble decorations on the facade, probably added by Jahangir. The principal features of this exquisite palace are the tiled decorations on the front wall, the square domed hall just

inside the entrance, and the grand central court which, as Carleylle maintained, 'is entirely Hindu in character. . . . But the stone roof or ceiling of these pillared halls is the most remarkable feature about it.' The roof of the central compartment 'is supported most curiously by stone cross-beams', carved

Below : *Entrance to the Samman Burj, with its central fountain. Bottom: The interior of the Moti Masjid.*

with mythical serpents. 'It is altogether a wonderfully constructed roof—a wonder of constructive ingenuity—unique and without parallel in its design.' The inspiration, however, as Cunningham points out, are the roofs in the Man Mandir Palace in

Overleaf : *An aerial view of Fatehpur Sikri, Akbar's capital for fifteen years, built in thanksgiving for the birth of heirs to the throne of Hindustan.*

Cenotaphs surround the marble memorial to Salim Chishti's tomb, the only building made entirely of marble in Fatehpur Sikri. Today, women crowd this cenotaph to the saint who had promised an heir to Akbar, in the hope that their prayers here will grant them a similar boon.

Gwalior. Akbar had already summoned the greatest singer of the age, Tan Sen, to his court from Gwalior. He was greatly influenced by his Rajput wife from Amber, and it is more than likely that she was behind his decision to build palaces in local styles. In Carleylle's opinion the bas-reliefs of birds, ducks, parrots and fruits were equalled for artistic inspiration and technical mastery only by some of the ancient Buddhist decorative panels.

The fort was the hub of life in the capital and the source of the imperial *firmans* to governors far and near. Finch, who spent nearly two years in Agra with Hawkins, trying unsuccessfully to outwit the Portuguese at Jahangir's court, has left a vivid description of the conduct of the emperor's business. Near the west gate, known as Hathi Pol from the elephants on either side, was the seat of the Kazi or chief justice and the office of the Vizier or revenue minister, who 'sits

every morning some three hours, by whose hands pass all matters of rents, grants, lands, *firmans*, debts, etc.' Hathi Pol was thus a place of public concourse, the closest of the four gates to the old city. Amar Singh gate to the south is the only one now open. The fort's store of ordnance was kept towards the north gate, while the fourth gate 'is to the river, the Dersane (Darshani) leading into a fair court extending amongst the river, in which the king looks forth every morning at sun-rising which he salutes, and then his nobles resort to their *tessillam*'.

Just outside the Darshani gate the emperor at noon 'looketh forth to behold Tamashan (*tamasha*, or show) of fighting elephants, lyons, buffles, killing of deare with leopards'. Once a week these blood sports gave way to the bloodier business of the execution of condemned men.

It is typical of Akbar's admiration for bravery that he honoured Jaimal and Patta,

the heroic defenders of Chittor, by placing their statues at Hathi Pol. A chivalric conqueror honoured his defeated foe. They were still there when Finch visited Agra.

Shah Jahan started work on his palaces in the fort soon after he secured the throne. Mumtaz Mahal died in 1631 while he was at Burhanpur in the Deccan. Her body was brought to Agra the following year. By then his architects and craftsmen had gained enough experience for him to confidently embark on his greatest project—the Taj Mahal. Work began almost immediately and continued until the mausoleum was completed 22 years later.

Shah Jahan's passion for building and great wealth do not adequately explain the astonishing outburst of architecture and the decorative arts during his reign. The perfectionists who so cunningly played with light and shade on dazzling white marble were heirs to the same tradition of excellence

as the stone cutters whose fame induced Timur to take some of them away with him over two centuries earlier to decorate his dazzling monuments in Samarqand. Nevertheless the Agra Fort pre-eminently expresses Akbar's majestic sense of empire. Its towering red sandstone walls contain the most sumptuous of all Mughal palaces, yet it will always remain the great red fort of Akbarabad. For sheer presence it has no rival in India.

FATEHPUR SIKRI

Scarcely 40 kilometres west of Agra, a thin spine of rock springs from the flat alluvial plain. It is the first outcrop of the Aravalli hills which, further north, girdle the seven pre-British cities of Delhi. All of them, except the last, are more ancient than even the old Rajput fort of Badalgarh and its contemporary, the Rajput town of Sikri at

Within Salim Chishti's tomb, with its stone-pierced screen, Akbar decorated the cenotaph chamber with lapis lazuli, mother-of-pearl and topaz. The actual mosque is located to one side of this complex approached through a triumphal gateway, the Buland Darwaza, that the Emperor ordered after his return from a successful campaign in the Deccan.

Right : *Panch Mahal, to one side of Anup Talao, was a pavilion Akbar reserved for his favourite consorts. The building, five storeys high, consists of 176 columns, no two of which, barring pairs, are alike.*
Below : *The facade of Salim Chishti's tomb reflected in the water tank of the Jama Masjid courtyard where Akbar is believed to have offered the Friday prayers in lieu of the head priest.*

the foot of Sikri hill.

In 1572 Akbar left his great fort at Agra. His son Jahangir wrote in his memoirs that his revered father, 'considering the village of Sikri, which was the place of my birth, lucky for him, made it his capital'. Akbar was then in his fortieth year. He was the most powerful of any of the country's rulers. It was time for a different kind of conquest—of wresting a complete new capital from the

rock of the Aravalli hills as an offering to the saint whose blessings had enriched his life with three sons.

Akbar set to work with the kind of devouring energy that had already won him outstanding military victories. In time the new capital became the hub of his empire, the scene of religious debates with men of all faiths and the place from where, in 1579, he promulgated his conceptually daring though short-lived religion of *Sulh-i-Kul* or complete concord. In 1574 he named it Fatehpur, a place of victory, to commemorate his sensational dash across the desert to complete the conquest of Gujarat. The creation of a totally new imperial complex, with thousands of officials, retainers, troopers and all the panoply of empire, called for imagination, masterly handling of resources and rare creative vision. Qualities which Akbar had in abundance.

When the Jesuits, Monserrate and his companion, arrived at the court in 1580, Akbar was still building, putting the finishing touches, perhaps, to the choicest buildings of all—those around Anup Talao and the mysterious elegance of the interior of the Diwan-i-Khas. 'Zelaldinus (Jalal-ud-din Muhammad Akbar),' says Monserrate, 'is so devoted to building that he sometimes himself quarries along with other workmen. Nor does he shrink from watching, and even practising, for the sake of amusement, the craft of an ordinary artisan.' He might well have tried his hand with hammer and chisel, but the brilliant reliefs that adorn Fatehpur's finest creations were quite clearly the work of master craftsmen whose skills were an inheritance from an unknown number of past generations.

There is little doubt that the creator of this bustling red sandstone city himself devised the layout of the imperial complex dominating the hill. We are told by Akbar's biographer that the great amirs and others, 'and the public generally, made dwellings for themselves . . .'. But nothing was allowed to get out of hand. Abu'l-Fazl describes in detail the trappings of the imperial camp. The similarities suggest that it was this camp which was reproduced in stone in the new capital. Akbar made skilful use of the jagged features of the Aravalli hills. 'The elaborate web of forms yielded to the asymmetries of the natural setting. . . . Red sandstone and mortar, annealed by age, in forms that are neither distinctively Islamic in conception nor entirely indigenous in execution, but an outstandingly successful blend of both, enfold the spine of the hill with a sensitivity to the environment rarely achieved in the long history of town planning in the Indian peninsula.'

The place of honour on the summit of the hill was given to the tomb of the saint, Salim Chishti, who died in 1574 soon after his imperial *murid* (disciple) made him the offering of his new capital. The exquisite resting place Akbar built for him was chastely veneered with white marble by Akbar's son, Jahangir. Its beauty is enhanced by its being placed in a setting of subdued rock and red sandstone, not quite in the centre of the surrounding courtyard. The western end of the courtyard is occupied by an exceptionally beautiful mosque. Built wholly in the ornate style, it is the real glory of Akbar's architecture in Fatehpur. Buland Darwaza, the imposing gateway completed in 1576, harmoniously combines massive solidity with such delicate features as a filigree of cupolas and an arrangement of *chhattris* (kiosks) breaking the skyline. Surprisingly its otherwise dominating presence enhances the beauty of the diminutive tomb instead of overshadowing it. A message, characteristic of its eclectic creator, adorns the façade in fine lettering: 'Jesus, Son of Mary (on whome be peace), said: The world is a bridge, pass over it but build no house upon it. Who hopes for an hour, hopes for eternity. The world is an hour. Spend it in prayer, for the

Left : Birbal's palace, made of sandstone, is richly carved in the Hindu tradition, and is one of Fatehpur Sikri's most beautiful residential buildings. Strangely, it forms an integral part of Akbar's harem complex: was it, therefore, his residence, or has it been so named because he helped design it? **Below** *: The facade of Sikri's Diwan-i-Khas, Akbar's special chamber for private meetings. Was it from here that he watched a game of chess being played in the courtyard, with dancing girls forming the 'live' pieces?*

rest is unseen.'

East of the courtyard, and a little lower on the hill, in modest submission as it were, lies what remains of the imperial complex. The buildings consist of three distinct groups—the palaces, the seraglio and the royal offices, with the emperor's Daulat Khana (Abode of Fortune) as the focus of the town plan. No one could enter without the emperor's express permission. The

Khwabgah, or sleeping chamber, was on the floor above. At first light, the emperor gave *darshan* to those who had collected outside. 'His Majesty', Abu'l-Fazl notes, then 'allows the attendants of the harem to pay their compliments. During this time various matters of worldly and religious import are brought to the notice of his majesty. . . .' Thence he proceeded to the Diwan-i-Am, or hall of public audience, to disburse justice.

On the way the emperor walked past Anup Talao (Peerless Pool), to which there can be little doubt he returned at the end of the day to view the dances of the *kanchanis* and hear the melodies of the unmatched musician of the age, Tan Sen.

But Akbar was pre-eminently an emperor concerned with ruling over people and territories, and only secondarily concerned with his own comfort. This order of concern comes out very clearly in the arrangement of buildings. 'It is hard', says Monserrate, 'to exaggerate how accessible he makes himself to all who wish audience of him. For he creates opportunities almost every day for any of the common people to see him and converse with him; and he endeavours to show himself pleasant-spoken and affable rather than severe to all who come to speak with him. . . .' The court, he continues, 'is always thronged with multitudes of men of every type', for Akbar 'is specially remarkable for his love of keeping great crowds of people around him'.

The principal place where he gave *darshan* to these multitudes was the Diwan-i-Am. The British made a road through it leading to the tomb of the saint on the summit of the hill. Though marred by this wholly unnecessary improvement, the place of public audience still retains its dignity and amplitude. Rings on the upper courses indicate that it was covered by cloth screens, and thus converted into a vast assembly hall.

The purpose of the remarkable chamber which has been called the Diwan-i-Khas, or hall of private audience, remains a mystery. W. H. Siddiqui has suggested that the superbly chiselled column radiating to the four corners was a *satun-i-adl*, or column of justice, from the top of which Akbar made important pronouncements. Akbar remained something of a mystery: none of his contemporaries were able to fathom the mystical depths of his mind.

Mystery also surrounds the purpose of the five-storeyed Wind-Tower. It catches currents of air from all directions. In Akbar's conception, however, this irregular open pyramid was more likely to have been a place of contemplation than one of pleasure. His own tomb bears a strong resemblance to the mysterious Panch Mahal. Though Persian in conception, it is entirely Indian in execution. Each succeeding level is placed asymmetrically and no two columns are exactly alike. Most of the motifs are Hindu in inspiration, suggesting that Akbar encouraged his workmen to make Fatehpur a vast canvas which they filled with works of genius. Here, in the Panch Mahal, they responded nobly, creating, as Rizvi and Flynn say, 'a veritable museum of styles'.

Anup Talao seems like a miniature stone and water charbagh with the central pavilion replacing the Hauz-i-Kausar. The whole complex of pavilions and pool were adorned by the finest of all the reliefs left to posterity by the stone carvers of Fatehpur. Floral designs alternate with arabesques with a fluency found only in the most elaborate wood carvings. As Abu'l-Fazl comments: 'Clever workmen chisel it so skilfully as no turner could with wood, and their works vie with the picture book of Mani (the great painter of the Sassanides).' The interior is completely covered with carvings of pastoral scenes, with animals and birds appearing as if in their own habitat.

The seraglio, to the north-west of the emperor's palace, is perhaps the most diverse and culturally significant of all the buildings

Facing page : An aerial view of Buland Darwaza, the southern gateway to the Jama Masjid. One of Akbar's greatest constructions at Fatehpur Sikri, it is reached by a flight of steps that rise forty feet high. The gateway, visible from all around as the tallest structure in the city, is topped with a delicate filigree of cupolas.

in Fatehpur. While respect for Islamic tradition fashioned the *mahals* of Akbar's mother and aunt, provision being made for the small Nagina Masjid for their use, the other palaces were apparently intended for Akbar's Hindu wives. Closest to his own Diwankhana-i-Khas is the Sunehra Makan or Golden Abode. This was clearly the palace of the Amber princess who was given the name Mariam Zamani, or Mariam of the Age. The interior was covered with paintings, many of them in gold. Sadly, they are now almost too faded to make out. As the mother of the heir, Prince Salim, Mariam Zamani was unquestionably the most influential of the ladies of the court.

South-west of the golden house is the Shabistan-i-Iqbal or principal Haram Sarai, a kind of dormitory occupied by Akbar's other Hindu wives. It is popularly known as Jodha Bai's Mahal, and is a world in itself. Apartments surround the courtyard where the princesses observed their own religious practices. The most striking feature of this *mahal* is the pair of blue-tiled rectangular roofs which still retain much of their original brilliance. Adjoining it is the Hawa Mahal, a screened pavilion for the enjoyment of the ladies. From here they could descend along screened passages to Hathi Pol gate to enjoy the cooling presence of Sikri lake. This, alas, has long since been drained and taken over for cultivation.

The palace known as Birbal's Mahal, the name of Akbar's boon companion and teller of droll stories, was obviously intended for the two senior ladies. It occupies the most prized position of all the palaces in Fatehpur. The excellence of its architecture and refinement of the decoration have rightly earned it F. W. Smith's encomium as the finest of the domestic buildings in the capital.

Fatehpur may lack the rugged strength of Agra Fort. Most of the buildings which still exist owe their preservation to the foresight of the imaginative and forceful Viceroy, Lord Curzon, at the turn of the last century. Though many of the buildings which have been preserved are carved in fantastic forms, and the surfaces chiselled in patterns of breathtaking intricacy, there is no trace in Akbar's city of the luxurious aestheticism of his son Jahangir or the often florid opulence of Shah Jahan.

All the rest has disappeared. Much of it has been pounded into the roads built by the British to maintain their empire, and a great deal more converted into the myriad humble dwellings built after the city was abandoned. Stone and mortar withstood the ravages of time but fell victim to the cupidity and folly of man.

Akbar left Fatehpur in 1586 to crush an incipient rebellion in Afghanistan. The northern part of the empire demanded his attention so he had to make Lahore his base for 14 years. He returned only briefly in 1601 while on his way to the Deccan. The reasons for Akbar's abandonment of the dream city are the subject of endless controversy. The plain fact is that the exigencies of empire took Akbar away, and his successors had their own interests. Jahangir camped in the safety of Fatehpur in 1619 while plague ravaged the great city of Agra. Though the devotion of the caretakers has saved the mosque and tomb and most of the imperial complex, hardly anything else remains of Akbar's original offering to the saint. The two exceptions are Todar Mal's *baradari*, some way off, and Hada Rani's Mahal, which is slung along the city walls towards Ajmer.

Facing page: A devout pilgrim catches up on his reading in the shadow of a fretwork screen at the Taj Mahal.

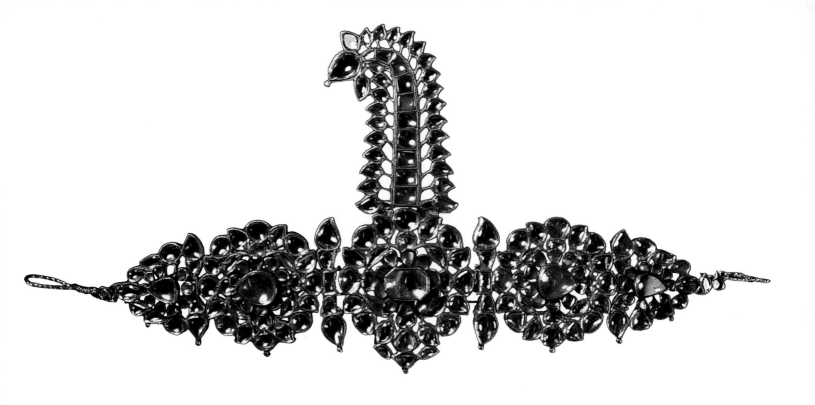

The Taj Mahal

Without doubt, the Taj Mahal ranks as the most perfect building in the world, flawlessly proportionate, built entirely of marble. Never before or since has mankind seen a structure of such enduring beauty. Ordered by Emperor Shah Jahan to commemorate the memory of his dearly loved wife, it is in reality his gift to the human race.

'The Lady of the Taj' was one of the three remarkable imperial consorts who created an imperishable niche for themselves in the history of the Mughal empire. All three were Persian. The first was Hamida Bano Begum who, when barely 15, was married to Humayun in the wilds of Sind and sustained the fugitive emperor with the solace of her companionship throughout his 15-year exile. The second was Nur Jahan whose intelligence and beauty so enslaved Jahangir that he virtually committed the empire to her care. The last of the three was Arjumand Bano Begum, who was given the name Mumtaz Mahal. Her devotion to her husband, the emperor Shah Jahan, inspired

the finest mausoleum ever created by the art of man.

When Shah Jahan moved his huge camp to the Deccan to deal with Khan Jahan Lodi's rebellion, the empress went with him. While the emperor was at Burhanpur, Mumtaz Mahal died giving birth to her fourteenth child. According to two contemporary authorities, when she knew the end was near she sent her elder daughter Jahanara to call the emperor. She entreated him to take good care of their children after she had left this world. The grief-stricken emperor gazed into her eyes as she died on 28 June 1631. The body was laid in a temporary grave, but was taken to Agra by Prince Shuja and a

Facing page : Emperor Shah Jahan, the greatest of the Mughal builders, has left behind an enduring legacy of buildings, whether in the apartments of Agra Fort, in the new city of Shahjahanabad in Delhi, or in the mausoleum he raised to the memory of his wife, the Taj Mahal. Above : An excellent quality of craftsmanship marks out this 'sarpech' or jewelled brooch worn on turbans.

Right : *Visitors shelter from rain in the portals of the mosque of the Taj Mahal.*
Below : *Muslim women pay homage to the empress in whose memory the world's most beautiful mausoleum has been raised. Islam decrees that a woman who dies in childbirth is given the same status as a martyr, and that her cenotaph be designated a place of pilgrimage.*

ambassador and leading nobles, followed by alms giving. Help to the indigent became an annual feature. A woman who died in childbirth was regarded as a *shaheed* (martyr) and her tomb an *urs* (place of pilgrimage). When the tomb was complete, a divine from Mecca conducted a solemn ceremony. Prayers were offered and recitations from the Koran were constantly repeated in the halls surrounding the cenotaph chamber, an observance that continues to this day.

When Shah Jahan died in 1666 his body was brought from the Samman Burj (Jasmine Tower) in the fort and laid beside his wife. In keeping with convention the actual graves are placed in an underground chamber while memorial cenotaphs are replicated in the vaulted chamber directly above, with the empress in the centre, exactly following the precedent in Itmad-ud-Daulah's tomb.

Mausoleums such as the Taj Mahal were very much more than mere burial chambers. As Fergusson points out, 'during the lifetime of the founder, the central building is called a *baradari* or festal hall, and is used as a place of recreation and feasting by him and his friends. After his death the purpose is changed; he is interred beneath the central dome and sometimes his favourite wife lies beside him.' Since the Taj was not built in the life time of Mumtaz Mahal, it could hardly have served as a festal hall and soon after its completion Shah Jahan himself was incarcerated in the Agra fort. However, as a mausoleum, it is of incomparable beauty.

The choice of the site was in itself an artistic decision. Viewed from the Samman Burj in the fort, which is from where the emperor saw it, it becomes clear that Shah Jahan planned it as a riverside *rauza* (tomb set in a garden). This was an arrangement much favoured by the Mughals. Humayun's tomb in Delhi (from where the river has retreated) and at least two surviving tombs in Agra, Itmad-ud-Daulah and Chini-ka-

favourite maid servant. Shah Jahan arrived in Agra five months later on 10 June 1632. Once again the body was laid in a temporary grave in Raja Jai Singh's garden. According to a *firman* of 18 December 1633, the emperor gave Raja Jai Singh four *havelis* (mansions) as compensation for the garden.

Shah Jahan returned just in time for Mumtaz Mahal's first death anniversary. It was celebrated by a feast for the Persian

Rauza—(which has the added distinction of being the only completely tile covered mausoleum in Agra) are all tombs set in gardens.

Who was the architect of the Taj? Western writers, under the spell of the Italian renaissance, at first put forward the name of a petty Venetian jeweller, Geronimo Veroneo, who died in Lahore in 1640, 14 years before the Taj was completed. His unpretentious gravestone makes no claim of his having had anything to do with the Taj. After this canard was exposed another took its place, in the mid-nineteenth century, in a Persian manuscript written at the instance of the European principal of a local college. It claimed that the architect was Isa Muhammad Effendi, who was said to have been sent by the Sultan of Turkey to assist the emperor. Colonel Sleeman, who had been in India since 1810, confidently asserted in his *Recollections* that the palm should be given to Austin of Bordeaux who, inconveniently for Sleeman, actually died in 1632, before work started on the Taj.

None of these early foreign authorities credited India with the expertise necessary for the construction and decoration of such a fine building. However, there is convincing documentary and epigraphic evidence that the architect was Ustad Ahmad Lahori. He was the Mimar-i-Kul or chief architect.

However, disproportionate importance is given to the identity of the architect for the practice in India at the time was for the emperor to appoint one of his amirs to coordinate the work of all the designers who produced the approved plan. It will be recalled that Qasim Khan was in charge of the construction of the Fort. We are told by the *Badshah Nama* that two high ranking amirs, Abdul Karim and Makramat Khan, were appointed to supervise the work of architects and builders.

The Mughal emperors were men of unusually good taste, and abundantly blessed

Left : The entrance to the Taj Mahal is a high sandstone gateway decorated with marble and topped with cupolas.
Below : A 'charbagh' or quadrangular garden surrounds the Taj Mahal, and a waterway with fountains leads to the monument. The lavish use of marble needs the relief of the gardens to absorb its dazzling impact.

with the means of giving expression to their vision of the beautiful. Shah Jahan's forte was the perfection of architectural form and refreshment of decoration. While competent persons were entrusted with the practical tasks, there seems little doubt that the inspiration for the Taj was essentially his own. A verse composed by Shah Jahan, and inscribed on the tomb, includes the revealing lines:

Overleaf : The devout gather to pray at the rauza or tomb of Empress Mumtaz Mahal.

Right and below : The Taj Mahal is a building of the most perfect proportions, and from all four sides, looks the same. The large entrance to the cenotaph chamber below is topped with a dome 237 feet (95 metres) high. Slender minarets and smaller domes arrange forms in a pleasing manner where no detail is superfluous, or excessive.

The builder could not have been of this earth,
For it is evident that the design was given to him by heaven.

The recipient of this heavenly inspiration could have been none other than the emperor himself. Ustad Ahmad Lahori and his associates were the agency through whom Shah Jahan gave form to the design 'given him by heaven'.

When work started in 1632 the finest builders, artisans and workmen flocked to Agra from all over Hindustan and West Asia. Ismail Khan of Turkey designed the two-shell dome. Passages from the Koran inscribed in Nashk characters on different parts of the monument, such as the main entrance to the tomb itself, are the work of the celebrated calligrapher, Amanat Khan Shirazi. The master-mason was Muhammad Hanif from Baghdad, and Kayam Khan, the pinnacle maker, was from Lahore. According to records found by Havell in the Imperial Library, then at Calcutta, the five principal mosaic workers were Hindus.

No detailed accounts of the cost have been preserved, nor of how the cost was met. There does not seem to have been a special levy of the kind Akbar imposed for the fort. Apart from an occasional foray in the Deccan, the empire had enjoyed a long spell of peace. The total cost was not beyond the enormous accumulated wealth of the emperor's treasury. When Bulganin and Khruschev visited India in 1955 the ebullient Khruschev asked me what the Taj had cost. I was ready with an answer. He brushed it aside saying that it was a product of slave labour. I made a spirited reply about the tradition of excellence of Indian craftsmen, but he did not appear convinced.

Records have recently come to light of payments being made for Makrana marble. Two special officers were posted there who regularly made payments from the imperial treasury. This information contradicts the purveyors of rumours that marble and other materials were supplied by vassal states without payment. It is quite likely, however, that the *nazranas* (offerings) of visiting idolatries were put to use.

The *Tarikh-i-Taj Mahal* gives details of the sources of the precious and semi-precious stones used for decoration, along with prices. For example, jasper came from the Punjab, carnelian from Baghdad, amethysts from Persia and sapphires from Sri Lanka—the list reads like the inventory of a jeweller in Delhi's Chandni Chowk today; there has been no change in the last three hundred and fifty years.

AN ENGINEERING MARVEL

For an empire with its vast resources, the actual construction of the Taj was very much more than assembling the finest talent and materials. Everything required had to be collected at the site, cut to size, finished and each piece placed exactly in place.

How was all this done? There is a tradition, impossible to dismiss, that a scale model was prepared for Shah Jahan's approval. That there were also detailed drawings can be inferred from the continuation of the work no matter where the emperor was. One of the original drawings of the Taj was last seen in 1916 in the possession of one Sharaf-ud-Din, whose ancestor was an architect in the emperor's service. Shah Jahan himself moved to Delhi in 1638, ten years before the mausoleum was completed, to start construction on his next project, the construction of Shahjahanabad. An Arabic inscription on the main gateway of the Taj reads: 'The end with the help of God' and gives the year of completion as the equivalent of 1648. The forecourt and its ancillaries took another five years.

Twenty thousand workmen applied themselves to the various construction tasks. The existence of mounds and depressions in the neighbourhood indicate that the small bricks used were burnt as close as possible, evidently to minimise problems of transport and supervision. Semi-precious stones were relatively easy to bring to the site, but marble and sandstone were not so easy to cart. When Manrique visited Bayana in 1640, he came across blocks of marble being taken to Agra. Some of these 'were of such unusual

Left and below : The mausoleum is based on a pattern of squares and circles, and the main body of the tomb comprises of a perfect square that is 186 feet (57 metres) on all sides. The square structure rises to a height of 108 feet (32 metres). The terrace on which the structure rests is a square 313 feet (95 metres) and extends from the mosque at the western end to the guest house in the east.

size and length that they drew the sweat of many powerful teams of oxen and fierce-looking, big-horned buffaloes, which were dragging enormous, strongly made wagons, in teams of twenty or thirty animals'. We are also told that no less than 1,14,000 cartloads of sandstone were hauled from nearby Fatehpur Sikri.

Tavernier, the French jeweller who visited Agra in the early years of construction, and

later when it was complete, heard the obviously exaggerated report that the scaffoldings alone cost more than the entire work, 'because, from want of wood, they as well as the supports of arches, had all to be made of brick'.

Shah Jahan, it is said, solved the problem of removing the scaffoldings by letting it be known that people who removed the bricks could keep them. The whole thing disappeared as if by magic and the Taj Mahal stood revealed in all its beauty.

It has been calculated that the walls of the cenotaph chamber carry a load of 8.02 metric tonnes per square foot, while the dome, as it rests on its drum, weighs 12,192.56 tonnes. How is this massive weight dispersed? The weight of the monument rests on arched vaults supported by a series of brick-lined wells sunk below the plinth. Rubble and hydraulic lime were rammed into the wells forming a solid foundation resting on

bedrock below. Similar wells were sunk in the river-front along the Taj to protect it from erosion and floods. There is also a suggestion that the river was trained to run west to east from the fort, creating enchanting vistas which consoled Shah Jahan during his last imprisonment.

PROPORTIONS

The experience of the Taj is essentially aesthetic, its dimensions creating its faultless harmony. Nothing is out of place, disproportionate or vulgar. The Mimar-i-Kul kept three requirements in mind as he planned the mausoleum: those of a *rauza* or tomb set in a riverside garden, an *urs* or place of pilgrimage and a festal hall for the emperor, with an appurtenant bazaar and place for alms giving. Above all a place of honour had to be found for the mosque. Ustad Ahmad Lahori adopted a simple layout

Facing page : One of the side arches that replicates the arch of the main entrance–the perfect arch highlighted with floral inlay and calligraphy.
Above: People atop the entrance parapet; the decorations are never overpowering, and ensure that the white marble mined in Makrana, does not dazzle.
Overleaf : A close-up of the onion-shaped dome resting on the square base plinth of the Taj Mahal.

Preceding pages : The Taj Mahal, constructed entirely of white marble, was twenty-two years in the making, and used a labour-force of twenty thousand workers. The central mausoleum stands on a terrace on the four corners of which are slender minarets that have been built with a slight outwards incline.

Above : The roof of the mosque that is part of the Taj Mahal complex, a red sandstone structure that helps lend visual balance to the enclosed gardens that separate the mosque and guest house from the marble mausoleum.

Facing page : The mosque is lavishly decorated, the sandstone exhibiting inlay and relief work to parallel that on the Taj Mahal.

to meet these requirements.

A large rectangular area roughly 579.12 metres long and 304.80 metres broad was set apart between the *qasba* of Tajganj and the river's edge. This was divided into two, the smaller for the forecourt and the larger for the *charbagh* and tomb. The visitor will immediately be struck by the sheer grandeur of the main gateway as he passes from the forecourt to the *charbagh*. It is a magnificent example of Persian design, topped by a coronal of entrancing beauty.

The apsed entrance, repeated at the back, is framed by marble bands inscribed in black slate with Koranic texts, the letters so fashioned that, standing on the ground, they appear to be of uniform size. The gateway opens into a vaulted chamber decorated with a network of designs in white stucco on a red background. Similar work decorates the vaults of the mosque and *Mehman Khana* (Guest House) flanking the tomb.

From the gateway right up to the plinth of the tomb is the *rauza* which is symbolic of the Bagh-i-Adan (Garden of Eden) of the Islamic paradise. It consists of an elevated central pool in dazzling white marble, with four water channels radiating to the points of the compass. The east-west channels terminate at *Naubat Khanas* (Music Houses) where musicians greeted the emperor on his weekly visits to the tomb.

Appropriately, the Bagh-i-Adan was meant to be a fruit and flower garden, thus providing an income to maintain the *khadims* (caretakers). Lawns and flowering trees replaced the original garden at the turn of the last century, with the result that the impact of the Taj is a shade more explicit than it was meant to be.

The tomb's plinth, at 5.5 metres, is a distinct improvement on Humayun's tomb where it is nearly a metre and a half higher. A higher plinth would have added an

unconscionable weight to the foundations and detracted from the river view. This was probably the deciding factor.

A narrow stairway brings the visitor face to face with the supremely beautiful entrance to the tomb. Stalactites carry the soffit to the point of the arch, the whole framed by marble bands inscribed in black slate with Koranic texts by the great master, Amanat Khan Shirazi. Evidence has been found that he also designed the inscriptions in Akbar's tomb at Sikandara.

Pietra dura inlay adorns the spandrels in flowing designs. Slender pilasters with black and yellow chevron tasselations spring upwards along the quoins to end in open lotuses, each crowned with a tiny dome and finial.

A single example will suffice to illustrate the care bestowed by the Mimar-i-Kul on seemingly minor points. The pilasters end above the parapet, though the recesses on either side end in lower parapets, permitting views of the corner *chhattris* which are only gradually covered as the tomb is approached. The discriminating visitor will take delight in discovering similar instances of attention to detail elsewhere. For example, the corners of the square structure are chamfered to provide additional planes for decoration, to relieve angularity and to relate the minarets to the whole ensemble in a way that would not have been quite so happy had the structure remained a perfect square.

Unquestionably, the dome is the tomb's crowning achievement. Its evolution from the rather squat Lodi feature, through the more elevated dome in Humayun's tomb to the perfect globe of the central segment in the Taj is its ultimate expression. Inside, the soffits soar to a height of 24.5 metres, leaving an immense hollow between the two shells, thus creating internal and external proportions of the purest harmony. The

highly successful mingling of Persian and indigenous features is demonstrated in the relation of the dome to its four attendant *chhattris* without the least suggestion of congestion. A single *chhattri* is placed over each chamfered corner, so that two *chhattris*, aligned with the corresponding minarets, transect the other diagonal through the centre of the drum supporting the dome. Detached from the funerary chamber, and yet integrally related to it, the four corner minarets, slender and tapering, nearly reach, without exceeding, the widest horizontal section of the dome. Thus they appear as the attendant corps de ballet, their simplicity enhancing the beauty of the centre piece, the tomb itself.

The internal arrangement of the Taj accords with the traditional Persian plan. Befitting his imperial status, Shah Jahan's cenotaph is much larger than the queen's, who preceded his release from life. The vault is drawn together in stalactite soffits, scarcely visible in the dim light. The rooms surrounding the cenotaphs radiate from the centre to the corners, converting the central chamber into an octagon. External light filters into the interior through double screens of marble, the spaces being filled with slightly milky glass. The whole interior is thus known as Aina Mahal or glass palace.

Marble reliefs of conventional motifs encircle the lowest course within the tomb and on the exterior, giving place above it to a display of pietra dura unrivalled for its elegance and restraint. These flowing inlays have the dual purpose of surface decoration and of breaking the dazzle of the sun. The pilasters, parapets and base of the dome are lightly decorated with formal designs of soft stone inlay, relieving any sense of decorative profligacy.

Ultimately all things lead, as they must, to the cenotaphs themselves. Fretted screens, exquisitely carved out of whole blocks of

Facing page: As the sun rises over the Taj Mahal, the light in the first blush of dawn colours it rose-hued. The architect of the building has been identified as Ustad Ahmad Lahori, though in the Mughal tradition it may be presumed that a number of architects and artistes contributed to its form supervised by a board of experts working from a wooden model. However, there can be no doubt that eventually it was Shah Jahan himself who gave it his vision and guided the final shape it was to take.
Above: The Taj Mahal framed in arches, as clouds lift off the river embankment on a winter morning.

white marble, set in frames of pietra dura inlay, form an octagon around the cenotaphs. This masterpiece alone took ten years to make. The air of hushed solemnity inside the screens, embalmed in the mottled light of Aina Mahal, is better experienced than described. There are few sights in the Taj to rival the approach to the cenotaphs through the open archway of the fretted marble screen. The austere emperor Aurangzeb allowed his father a more imposing stone than the empress', but Koranic texts are conspicuously absent from it.

Down below, in the mortuary chamber, Mumtaz Mahal's gravestone is inscribed with the ninety-nine names of Allah in highly stylised Nashk characters. All the artistry and skill of the designers is lavished on the beautifully proportioned marble graves. Agate, bloodstone, lapis lazuli, carnelian and other stones are cut and laid in floral arabesques and carpet designs with such precision that it is difficult, with the naked eye, to distinguish each piece. There are as many as thirty-one in the poppy and sixty-four in the large flower on the outer side of the arch in the screen enclosing the cenotaphs.

One of the *huffaz* reciting passages from the Koran may be persuaded to intone 'Allah-hu-Akbar', and the visitor must wait thirteen seconds for the echo to fade away in the domed vault. After this one may wish to preserve the effect by retracing one's steps to the forecourt, pondering the question of whether the Taj can survive the marauding hand of man and the penetrating acids of pollution.

At first man was the enemy. The Jats carried away silver from the main gateway in the mid-eighteenth century, along with other 'trophies' from Machhi Bhawan in the fort and Akbar's tomb in Sikandra. When Lord Lake occupied Agra in 1803 his dragoons stripped 44,000 *tolas* of pure gold which sheathed the finial of the Taj. Stones were gouged from their setting by British troops,

provoking a characteristic remark from Lord Curzon: 'It was not an uncommon thing for the revellers to arm themselves with hammer and chisel, with which they whiled away the afternoon by chipping out fragments of agate and carnelian from the cenotaphs of the Emperor and his lamented Queen.' As Viceroy, Curzon introduced protective legislation which saved the Taj and thousands of other monuments from further despoliation.

But who can prevent the air from bringing with it corrosive acids which eat into the Taj's Makrana marble? Steps have been taken to remove the hundreds of forges which sprang up all over the city, but the dangers of pollution have been compounded by the unwise decision to site a huge petrochemical complex on the Agra road from Mathura and unless care is exercised, we could end up losing one of the finest monuments within the country.

Facing page : The terrace on which the Taj Mahal stands, also support the four minarets, one at either end, which give the mausoleum its airy elegance. Overleaf : The Taj Mahal, as seen from fields across the river. The mosque and the guest house flank two sides; the entrance fronts a third; while on the fourth side is the river Yamuna.

CREDITS

Text Editors: Suhit K. Sen, B. N. Varma
Picture Editor: Pramod Kapoor
Typesetting: Monika Raj Malik, Fleming George P.

PHOTO CREDITS

Karoki Lewis: Cover inset (1), half title, title, Pages 8-9, 12-13, 33 (bottom), 36, 42, 43, 50-51,
56 (bottom), 57 (bottom), 58 (top and bottom), 70, 72 (bottom), 76 (top and bottom),
79, 86-87, 88, 89, 90, 91, 94-95.
D. N. Dube: Cover inset (1), Pages 4-5, 6-7, 14-15 (3 pix), 16-17, 20, 21, 26 (top and bottom),
27 (top and bottom), 37, 46-47, 54, 64 (top), 65(top), 69, 73 (top and bottom), 74-75, 77 (top), 80-81
Ashok Dilwali: Main cover, Pages 28-29, 33 (top), 34, 35, 38-39, 40, 41, 52, 53, 56 (top), 57 (top),
59 (top and bottom),
62, 63, 64(bottom), 65 (bottom), 72 (top), 77 (bottom), 78, 82-83, 84-85, 93
Pramod Kapoor: Pages 10-11, 24-25, 60-61, 66
Roli Books (P) Ltd.: Pages 32 (top and bottom)
National Museum: The following photographs come courtesy the National Museum: cover insets (2),
Pages 14-15 (4), 18, 19, 22 (top and bottom), 23 (top and bottom), 30, 31, 44 (6),
45, 48 (top and bottom), 49 (top and bottom), 55, 71